Sp

Travel Guia

Your Secret to Genuine Experiences in 2024

Florence Whitehead

Table of Contents

Introduction

Nestled in the heart of Dalmatia, where the Adriatic Sea meets the sun-kissed horizon, lies the timeless city of Split. This destination defies expectations, inviting wanderers into an enchanting tapestry woven with history, culture, and Mediterranean allure.

My journey through Split was more than a mere exploration; it was a dance with serendipity. Stepping onto the weathered cobblestones of Diocletian's Palace, I felt an undeniable energy, as if the stones whispered tales of emperors and epochs, an invitation to unlock the secrets of this living monument.

The sunsets in Split are a poetic spectacle, painting the sky with hues of amber and rose. Atop Marjan Hill, a panoramic view unfolded, connecting me to Split's past, present, and future. Navigating the city is an art form, a delightful maze revealing treasures at every turn—narrow alleys, hidden courtyards, and the rhythmic hum of Dalmatian songs in quaint cafes.

The warmth of Split's people is as vibrant as the bougainvillea adorning the facades. Croatians exude hospitality, sharing anecdotes in family-run konobas and along the Riva promenade. Dalmatian cuisine is a symphony of flavors, from peka-roasted lamb to fresh Adriatic seafood, offering a taste of Split's rich history.

Bacvice Beach's crystalline waters revealed why Split is an experience, not just a destination. The beaches, palm-fringed and lively, create an atmosphere of perpetual summer. The juxtaposition of ancient and modern is seamless, as witnessed in contemporary art galleries and the celebrated Split Summer Festival.

In conclusion, dear reader, a journey to Split is a step into a realm where history and modernity converge. The city's vibrant cultural scene and the welcoming embrace of its people create an atmosphere that is both timeless and pulsating with life. Let your adventure begin, for in Split, greatness awaits, and every step is a testament to the extraordinary beauty of exploration. The magic of Split, with its whispers of bygone eras and warm hospitality, awaits those fortunate enough to wander its storied streets.

Welcome to Split

Welcome to Split, an enduring treasure in the heart of Dalmatia, where the Adriatic Sea meets the sun-kissed horizon. This city surpasses expectations, offering an enthralling mix of history, culture, and Mediterranean charm.

Your journey in Split is more than exploration; it's a serendipitous dance. Sense the energy beneath your feet on the weathered cobblestones of Diocletian's Palace—a living monument that murmurs tales of emperors and epochs.

Sunsets in Split are a poetic spectacle, with hues of amber and rose painting the sky. From Marjan Hill, embrace a panoramic view connecting you to Split's past, present, and future. Navigating the city is an art form, revealing treasures in narrow alleys and the rhythmic hum of Dalmatian songs in quaint cafes.

Experience the vibrant warmth of Split's people, reflected in family-run konobas and along the lively Riva promenade. Indulge in the symphony of Dalmatian cuisine, from peka-roasted lamb to fresh Adriatic seafood, offering a taste of Split's rich history.

Bacvice Beach's crystalline waters reveal why Split is an experience, not just a destination. The beaches, palm-fringed and lively, create an atmosphere of perpetual summer. The seamless juxtaposition of ancient and modern unfolds in contemporary art galleries and the celebrated Split Summer Festival.

In conclusion, dear visitor, your journey in Split is a step into a realm where history and modernity converge. The city's vibrant cultural scene and warm hospitality create an atmosphere that is both timeless and pulsating with life. Begin your adventure, for in Split, greatness awaits, and every step is a testament to the extraordinary beauty of exploration. The magic of Split, with its whispers of bygone eras and warm hospitality, awaits those fortunate enough to wander its storied streets. Welcome to Split!

What's New in 2024

Embark on a journey through the latest offerings in Split for 2024, as this timeless city continues to evolve with captivating developments.

Modern Marvels: Discover a seamless blend of ancient and modern in Split. Contemporary structures enhance the skyline, adding a dynamic touch to the city's architectural narrative.

Cutting-Edge Cultural Scene: Immerse yourself in the expanding cultural tapestry with innovative art galleries and performances. The city embraces the future while honoring its storied past through the latest exhibits and events.

Culinary Delights: Indulge in the evolution of Dalmatian cuisine at trendy eateries. From chic cafes to avant-garde restaurants, savor inventive dishes that push the boundaries of flavor.

Sustainable Initiatives: Join Split in its commitment to sustainability. Explore eco-friendly practices integrated into daily life, from green spaces to initiatives supporting a cleaner Adriatic.

Tech-Friendly Exploration: Navigate the city with the latest tech enhancements. Interactive maps, virtual guides, and augmented reality experiences offer a tech-savvy approach to discovering hidden gems in Split.

Festivals and Events: Dive into the vibrant atmosphere of Split's festivals and events. From the renowned Split Summer Festival to cutting-edge celebrations, the city pulsates with life year-round.

Elevated Accommodations: Experience comfort and style in the newest wave of accommodations. Contemporary hotels and boutique stays cater to the modern traveler, providing a luxurious backdrop to your Split adventure.

Waterfront Wonders: The waterfront comes alive with new attractions. Stroll along revamped promenades, discover innovative installations, and relish the ever-present allure of the Adriatic Sea.

Sustainable Tourism Practices: Embrace responsible travel with initiatives focused on preserving Split's natural and cultural heritage. Join the city in its commitment to sustainable tourism practices for a fulfilling and eco-conscious visit.

Community Connection: Engage with the local community through immersive experiences. From cultural exchanges to grassroots initiatives, forge connections that go beyond the tourist surface and contribute to the heartbeat of Split.

In 2024, Split invites you to explore the latest chapters in its ever-evolving story. Embrace the new while cherishing the timeless charm that makes Split a destination like no other. Your adventure awaits in this city where history and modernity coalesce in a harmonious dance.

Itinerary

Split Itinerary: February 25

- Morning: Begin your day with a delightful breakfast at Caffe Bar Dujam, a local favorite. Immerse yourself in the ancient history of Diocletian's Palace, a UNESCO World Heritage Site. Explore its underground chambers and the well-preserved Peristyle Square (Peristil) [9998].

- Afternoon: For lunch, head to Restaurant Bajamonti and savor Mediterranean cuisine. Visit the imposing Cathedral of St. Dominus (Katedrala Svetog Duje). Take a leisurely walk along the Riva Promenade (Riva Split Waterfront) and enjoy the sea breeze.

- Evening: Dine at Zinfandel Food & Wine Bar, known for its elegant ambiance and excellent wine selection. Afterward, witness the majestic Gregory of Nin

(Grgur Ninski), a large bronze statue by Ivan Meštrović, and learn about its historical significance.

Split Itinerary: February 26

- Morning: Enjoy a hearty breakfast at Mazzgoon, a cozy spot with a variety of options. Venture to nearby islands, starting with the stunning Zlatni Rat Beach (Golden Horn) on the island of Brač, known for its unique shape and crystal-clear waters.

- Afternoon: For lunch, visit Olive Tree Dining & Clubbing and indulge in their fusion cuisine. Continue to the serene Solta Island, exploring charming villages and olive groves, or simply relax on one of its hidden beaches.

- Evening: Return to Split and dine at Morei, offering a blend of Dalmatian and international flavors. Conclude the day with a leisurely walk through lush Marjan Park (Marjan) [9990], enjoying panoramic views of the city and the Adriatic.

Split Itinerary: February 27

- Morning: Start with breakfast at Fabrique Pub, a trendy spot with a laid-back atmosphere. Embark on an early excursion to the mesmerizing Bisevo Blue Cave (Modra Spilja), where sunlight creates a magical blue glow.

- Afternoon: Head to the secluded Stiniva Cove, surrounded by towering cliffs. Enjoy a picnic from Tortuga Grill & Pub. Cruise to nearby Budikovac Island (Veliki Budikovac) and unwind on its pebble beach.

- Evening: Return to Split and dine at the Sanctuary Cantina, known for its innovative dishes. Take a guided tour of Split Old Town to discover hidden alleys and local stories under the evening lights.

Split Itinerary: February 28

- Morning: Enjoy breakfast at Café & Restaurant Lvxor Split, overlooking the city. Gear up for an exciting morning rafting or canoeing experience on the Cetina River, surrounded by lush forests and dramatic cliffs.

- Afternoon: Have a leisurely lunch at the BAZA food bar with good vibes. Post-lunch, visit the ancient ruins of Salona, exploring its archaeological park.

- Evening: For dinner, head to Jimmy Bar, a stylish venue with a diverse menu. Cap off the evening at the BOILER club and dining, enjoying live music and the vibrant nightlife of Split.

Split Itinerary: February 29

- Morning: Begin your last day with breakfast at Maduro Bar. Visit the intriguing Mestrovic Gallery (Galerija

Mestrovic), dedicated to the works of renowned Croatian sculptor Ivan Meštrović.

- Afternoon: Have a relaxed lunch at the SideBar, restaurant, sports, and music terrace. Spend the afternoon at the vibrant Bacvice Beach, known for its shallow waters and the traditional game of picigin.
- Evening: As the sun sets, enjoy a farewell dinner at Art Gallery Cafe Music Bar Split. Conclude the evening with a visit to Froggyland, a unique museum featuring over 500 stuffed frogs in various human poses, providing a quirky and memorable end to your time in Split.

Chapter One

Getting Started

Essential travel tips

Ensure a smooth and enjoyable journey to Split with these essential travel tips:

Currency Matters: Familiarize yourself with the Croatian kuna (HRK) exchange rate and keep some local currency for small purchases.

Language: While English is common, learning basic Croatian phrases can enhance your experience and connect you with locals.

Transportation Savvy: Use the efficient public transportation system, including buses and ferries, for city exploration. Taxis are available; agree on fares in advance.

Weather Awareness: Pack for Split's Mediterranean climate. Summers are hot and dry, and winters are mild. Check the forecast and pack sunscreen, a hat, and comfortable shoes.

Cultural Respect: Observe local customs. Dress modestly at religious sites and greet locals with a friendly "Dobar dan" (good day).

Safety First: While Split is generally safe, be wary of pickpockets in crowded areas. Secure your belongings, especially in markets and tourist spots.

Explore Off-Peak: Visit attractions early or during shoulder seasons (spring and fall) to avoid crowds.

Local Cuisine Exploration: Try traditional dishes like pasticada, peka-roasted lamb, and fresh seafood. Enjoy the lively atmosphere of the local konobas.

Sunscreen Essentials: Protect yourself from the intense Adriatic sun. Apply sunscreen regularly, stay hydrated, and seek shade during peak sunlight hours.

Connectivity: Ensure your phone is unlocked for local SIM cards or international roaming. Reliable internet access is useful for navigation.

Plan Island Hopping: Explore nearby islands like Hvar or Brac for a day trip. Check ferry schedules in advance for a smooth island-hopping experience.

Time Zone Reminder: Croatia follows Central European Time (CET). Adjust your schedule to make the most of your time in Split.

With these tips, your journey to Split promises to be memorable and stress-free. Embrace local culture, savor flavors, and explore the rich history of this enchanting Mediterranean city. Safe travels!

Packing Hacks for Split

Enhance your comfort and convenience with these savvy packing tips for your trip to Split:

Lightweight Layers: Pack breathable, versatile clothing for the Mediterranean climate. Opt for adaptable layers to stay comfortable in varying temperatures throughout the day.

Compact Footwear: Bring comfy walking shoes for city exploration and easy-to-slip-on flip-flops or sandals for beach visits.

Beach Essentials: Don't forget your swimsuit, sunscreen, and a beach towel for relaxation on the stunning Adriatic beaches.

Daypack Delight: Carry a compact daypack for daily explorations, perfect for storing water, snacks, sunscreen, and souvenirs.

Sun Protection Gear: Shield yourself with a wide-brimmed hat, sunglasses, and a reusable water bottle. Ensure high-SPF sunscreen for protection.

Adapter Basics: Pack a universal adapter for your devices. Croatia uses a standard European two-pin plug.

Tech Essentials: Bring a portable charger, camera, and lightweight e-reader for capturing moments and leisurely reading.

Smart Packing Cubes: Organize efficiently with packing cubes for easy access to your belongings.

Multipurpose Clothing: Opt for items that serve multiple purposes, like a versatile scarf for various uses.

Toiletry Tactics: Save space with travel-sized toiletries and consider solid options to comply with liquid restrictions during air travel.

Laundry Solutions: Pack a small laundry bag and travel-size detergent for a quick wash, ensuring clean clothes throughout your trip.

Compact First Aid Kit: Assemble a compact kit with essentials like bandages, pain relievers, and any necessary prescription medications.

Incorporate these packing hacks for a hassle-free exploration of Split's enchanting streets, beaches, and historical wonders. Enjoy your trip!

Chapter Two

Navigating Split

City Layout and Landmarks

Situated on the eastern shore of the Adriatic Sea, Split, Croatia, is a captivating coastal city that seamlessly integrates ancient charm with modern amenities.

- Diocletian's Palace:

The UNESCO-listed Diocletian's Palace, dating back to the 4th century, forms the city's core. Its well-preserved Roman architecture is surrounded by lively cobblestone streets hosting shops, cafes, and restaurants.

- Old Town (Historic Center):

Surrounding Diocletian's Palace, the Old Town is a labyrinth of alleys and squares. Key attractions include the Cathedral of Saint Domnius and the Peristyle, offering a glimpse into the city's rich history.

- Riva Promenade:

The vibrant Riva Promenade stretches along the waterfront, providing a scenic setting for leisurely strolls, seafront cafes, and open-air events.

- Marjan Hill:

To the west, Marjan Hill offers a serene escape with its forested park. Trails for hiking and biking lead to panoramic viewpoints, showcasing the beauty of Split and the Adriatic.

- Bacvice Beach:

East of the city center, Bacvice Beach is a sandy haven favored by locals and visitors alike. Known for its lively nightlife, it boasts beachside clubs and cafes.

Key Landmarks:

- Cathedral of Saint Domnius:

Nestled within Diocletian's Palace, this cathedral is a medieval masterpiece, featuring a bell tower that provides sweeping views of the city.

- Peristyle:

The central square of Diocletian's Palace, the Peristyle, is a hub for cultural events and live performances, surrounded by impressive columns.

- Gregory of Nin Statue:

Found near the Golden Gate, this iconic statue is believed to bring good luck when its toe is rubbed.

- Golden Gate and Silver Gate:

Well-preserved entrances to Diocletian's Palace, these gates showcase intricate details and Roman architectural finesse.

- Mestrovic Gallery:

Dedicated to sculptor Ivan Mestrovic's works, this gallery is housed in a villa with a picturesque garden.

With its blend of historical landmarks, vibrant streets, and natural wonders, Split beckons visitors to explore its unique fusion of past and present.

Public Transportation Guide

- Buses:

Explore Split and its outskirts through the city's extensive bus network. The main bus station, centrally located near the ferry terminal, serves as a vital hub for various routes.

- Local Transport Cards:

Enhance your public transportation experience with a local transport card. Load it with credit for use on buses, trams, and select ferries, offering discounted fares compared to single tickets.

- Trams:

While Split's tram network is limited to the city center, it provides a convenient option for short-distance travel and is known for its punctuality.

- Ferries:

Discover nearby islands and coastal towns via ferries departing from the main terminal near the Old Town. Ferries offer a scenic and popular means of exploring the Adriatic coastline.

- Taxi Services:

Taxis are readily available, either at designated stands or hailed on the street. Choose licensed taxis for fair pricing, and consider the availability of ride-sharing services.

- Walking and Biking:

With a compact city center, Split is highly walkable, and many attractions are within easy reach. Bike rental services are also available for those who prefer exploring on two wheels.

- Airport Shuttle:

Connect seamlessly between the city and Split Airport with shuttle services. These cost-effective shuttles provide a convenient link to the airport.

- Park and Ride:

Embrace the Park and Ride concept, where visitors can park on the outskirts and utilize public transportation to reach the city center, reducing congestion in the historic area.

- Car Rentals:

Enjoy flexibility by renting a car from several agencies operating in Split. This option allows you to explore the city and surroundings at your own pace.

- Real-Time Apps:

Optimize your journey with mobile apps offering real-time information on bus and ferry schedules, aiding efficient trip planning.

Navigating Split's public transportation system is user-friendly, providing diverse options for exploring the city and its scenic surroundings.

Chapter Three

Cultural Immersion

Historical Treasures

Discover Split's historical gems, a testament to its rich past shaped by diverse civilizations:

- Diocletian's Palace:

Built in the 4th century AD, this UNESCO-listed palace was Roman Emperor Diocletian's retirement haven. Explore its well-preserved structures, squares, and the iconic Peristyle.

- Cathedral of Saint Domnius (St. Duje):

Originally Diocletian's mausoleum, it was transformed into a cathedral housing Saint Domnius' remains. The cathedral's bell tower offers panoramic views, creating a captivating historical backdrop.

- Peristyle:

The vibrant heart of Diocletian's Palace, the Peristyle, surrounded by majestic columns, hosts cultural events and gatherings, adding a lively touch to the historical surroundings.

- Golden Gate and Silver Gate:

These well-preserved gates, adorned with intricate carvings, served as the main entrances to Diocletian's Palace, showcasing Roman architectural brilliance.

- Grgur Ninski Statue:

Near the Golden Gate, this statue of Grgur Ninski is a symbol of Split, where rubbing the toe promises good luck, adding a touch of local tradition to the historical narrative.

- Jupiter's Temple:

Nestled within Diocletian's Palace, this ancient Roman temple dedicated to Jupiter has evolved over time, now serving as a unique baptistery.

- Medieval Town Gates:

Encircling Split's Old Town, the Iron, Bronze, and Silver Gates each hold distinct historical significance, providing a glimpse into the medieval charm of the city.

- Ethnographic Museum Split:

Housed in a 16th-century palace, this museum unveils artifacts, offering insights into Split's cultural and historical evolution through the ages.

- City Museum of Split:

Residing in Papalic Palace, this museum unfolds Split's history via archaeological finds, historical documents, and art collections, adding depth to the city's narrative.

- Salona Archaeological Park:

Just beyond Split, Salona unveils the grandeur of Roman urban planning, with well-preserved amphitheaters, basilicas, and structures, providing a fascinating glimpse into ancient times.

These historical treasures, bursting with stories, contribute to Split's allure, inviting you to a journey through the ages and civilizations.

Local Cuisine and Dining Hotspots

Savor the coastal charm of Split with its diverse culinary offerings shaped by rich cultural influences. Here's a taste of traditional dishes and dining spots in the city:

Local Cuisine:

- Pasticada:

Indulge in slow-cooked beef marinated in wine and spices, often paired with gnocchi or pasta, for a hearty and flavorful experience.

- Brudet:

Delight in a fisherman's stew, a medley of fish, shellfish, and tomatoes seasoned with garlic, parsley, and Mediterranean herbs.

- Octopus Salad:

Refresh your palate with a light salad featuring tender octopus, potatoes, onions, and capers dressed in olive oil and lemon juice.

- Dalmatian Prosciutto (Pršut):

Relish thinly sliced air-dried ham, a local delicacy served with cheese, olives, and fresh bread.

- Black Risotto (Crni Rižot):

Experience the unique flavor of cuttlefish or squid ink in this rich black risotto—a seafood lover's delight.

- Pašticada:

Enjoy beef stewed in a flavorful sauce of red wine, prosciutto, and spices, paired with gnocchi or pasta.

- Fritule:

Indulge in small, deep-fried doughnuts flavored with brandy, citrus zest, and powdered sugar—a popular dessert or snack.

Dining Hotspots:

- Konoba Matejuska:

Feast on fresh seafood and local dishes in the traditional Dalmatian konoba near the fish market, offering a charming sea view.

- Bokeria Kitchen & Wine Bar:

Blend modern ambiance with Dalmatian flavors at Bokeria, renowned for its diverse menu and extensive wine selection.

- Tavern Fife:

Experience authentic Croatian dishes in a cozy setting at Tavern Fife, a favorite among locals and tourists for its generous portions and reasonable prices.

- Uje Oil Bar:

Explore Mediterranean-inspired cuisine at Uje Oil Bar, featuring olive oils, cheeses, and cured meats that showcase the region's flavors.

- Nostromo:

Delight in seafood specialties at Nostromo near the waterfront, offering fresh fish dishes and seafood platters.

- Dvor:

Dine elegantly within Diocletian's Palace at Dvor, where Mediterranean and Croatian cuisine meet, accompanied by picturesque views from the terrace.

- Zinfandel Food & Wine Bar:

Discover a modern dining experience at Zinfandel, offering a diverse menu of Croatian and international dishes and an extensive wine list.

- Uje Oil Bar and Trattoria Tinel:

Enjoy a blend of an oil bar and trattoria at Uje Oil Bar & Trattoria Tinel, offering olive oils and traditional Dalmatian dishes in a charming setting.

Embark on a gastronomic adventure in Split, immersing yourself in the culinary heritage that defines the region.

Festivals and events

Explore the lively cultural scene of Split through its diverse festivals and events, celebrating heritage, music, arts, and traditions.

- Split Carnival (Split Fasnik):

Dive into the vibrant pre-Lenten festivities with parades, masked balls, and street performances at the lively Split Carnival, where locals and visitors showcase elaborate costumes and masks.

- Split Film Festival:

Join filmmakers, producers, and cinema enthusiasts at the historic Split Film Festival, Croatia's esteemed platform for independent and international films.

- Days of Diocletian (Dane Dioklecijana):

Step back in time during the Days of Diocletian, an annual event transforming Split into a living Roman museum with reenactments, gladiator fights, and cultural performances.

- Ultra Europe Music Festival:

Immerse yourself in the beats of Ultra Europe, a global music extravaganza in Split featuring world-renowned DJs and electronic dance music acts.

- Split Summer Festival (Splitsko Ljeto):

Experience cultural richness at the Split Summer Festival, offering theater, opera, ballet, and classical music performances in historic venues like Peristyle and Diocletian's Palace.

- Days of Marjan (Dani Marjana):

Celebrate Marjan Hill's natural beauty with outdoor activities, cultural performances, and environmental initiatives, encouraging appreciation and preservation of green spaces.

- International Flower Fair (Međunarodni Sajam Cvijeća):

Wander through the vibrant city center during the International Flower Fair, a colorful display of flowers and plants enhancing Split's urban landscape.

- Split Christmas Market:

Embrace the holiday spirit at the Split Christmas Market in the Old Town, featuring local crafts, festive treats, and entertainment for all ages.

- Split International Shakespeare Festival:

Enjoy theatrical performances, workshops, and lectures honoring William Shakespeare at the Split International Shakespeare Festival, which attracts local and international artists and enthusiasts.

- Festival of the Mediterranean Film (Festival Mediteranskog Filma):

Immerse yourself in Mediterranean cinema at this festival, showcasing documentaries, feature films, and shorts that provide unique perspectives on Mediterranean culture and society.

These events infuse Split with a dynamic atmosphere throughout the year, offering a blend of cultural, artistic, and entertainment experiences.

Chapter Four

Outdoor Adventures

Beaches and Waterfront Escapes

Discover the coastal allure of Split through its exquisite beaches and waterfront retreats along the stunning Adriatic Sea.

- Bacvice Beach:

Just east of the city center, Bacvice beckons with its shallow, sandy shores—an ideal family-friendly destination. The beach exudes vibrancy with beachside cafes and the traditional game of picigin.

- Firule Beach:

Adjacent to Bacvice, Firule offers a tranquil escape with pebbly shores, providing a quieter alternative for those seeking a more relaxed beach experience.

- Kasjuni Beach:

Nestled on the southern slope of Marjan Hill, Kasjuni's pebble beach, embraced by pine trees, offers a serene setting and crystal-clear waters, making it a local favorite.

- Bene Beach:

On the western side of Marjan Hill, Bene welcomes families with a mix of pebbles and rocky areas. Set against a pine forest backdrop, it provides shade and a sense of seclusion.

- Znjan Beach:

Znjan stretches with a blend of pebbles and concrete, featuring beach bars, cafes, and sports facilities—a popular choice for both locals and tourists.

- Trstenik Beach:

Tucked in the eastern part of Split, Trstenik offers a local experience with a pebble beach surrounded by residential areas and a few nearby cafes and restaurants.

- Bene Park (Marjan Forest Park):

Beyond beaches, Marjan Hill transforms into a picturesque park with walking and biking trails, offering breathtaking views of the city and the sea. Secluded spots along the coastline invite those seeking a more private retreat.

- Matejuška Harbor:

Though not a typical beach, Matejuška Harbor near Diocletian's Palace charms with colorful boats, cafes, and seafood restaurants—a perfect spot for enjoying the sea breeze and sunset.

- Bene Cove:

A small, secluded cove near Bene Beach provides a quieter, more intimate waterfront experience for those seeking serenity.

- Žnjan Promenade:

Alongside the beach, Žnjan boasts a lengthy promenade adorned with bars, cafes, and restaurants—an inviting locale for a leisurely waterfront stroll.

Whether it's the sandy expanse of Bacvice or the secluded charm of Bene Cove, Split's beaches and waterfront areas promise diverse options for relaxation and enjoyment by the Adriatic Sea.

Hiking and nature trails

Explore the outdoor beauty of Split through its diverse hiking and nature trails, particularly around Marjan Hill and its environs:

- Marjan Hill Hike:

Discover the green oasis of Marjan Hill, west of the city center, with numerous hiking trails rewarding adventurers with panoramic views of Split, the Adriatic Sea, and nearby islands.

- Marjan Coastal Path:

Embrace the scenic beauty of the coastline along Marjan Hill, offering breathtaking sea views. This relatively easy walk through pine forests caters to all ages.

- Vidilica Viewpoint:

Accessible from Marjan Hill, Vidilica is a viewpoint boasting stunning panoramic views of Split and the surrounding islands—a delightful reward for hikers.

- Kasjuni-Milicevo Forest Trail:

Traverse the dense pine forest on Marjan Hill, experiencing a peaceful and shaded hiking journey that reveals the natural beauty of the hill.

- Bene Valley and Park:

Explore the lush vegetation surrounding Bene Beach, with well-marked paths suitable for both walking and jogging in the serene ambiance of Marjan Forest Park.

- Marjan Cave Exploration:

For the adventurous, Marjan Hill offers caves to explore, such as the popular Gospa od Špilice cave, adding an element of excitement to your hiking experience.

- Mosor Mountain Trails:

Northeast of Split, the Mosor mountain range provides challenging hiking trails with rewarding views of the Adriatic Sea, the city, and the countryside.

- Kozjak Mountain Trails:

To the northwest, Kozjak Mountain offers a variety of hiking trails with elevated viewpoints, providing panoramic vistas of Split and the islands.

- Klis Fortress Hike:

A short drive from Split, the hike to Klis Fortress atop a hill offers not only historical exploration but also picturesque views of the landscape.

- Sustipan Promenade:

Experience the tranquility of Sustipan on the southwestern tip of Split through a scenic promenade with sea views, historical charm, and serene spots for relaxation.

These trails cater to diverse fitness levels and preferences, inviting you to immerse yourself in the natural beauty and historical allure that surround Split.

Chapter Five

Nightlife and Entertainment

Trendy bars and clubs

Experience the vibrant and diverse nightlife of Split with these popular spots for entertainment and socializing:

- Central Cafe Bar:

Near Diocletian's Palace, this trendy bar boasts a modern ambiance, an extensive cocktail menu, and occasional live music performances for a relaxed and lively experience.

- To Je:

Located in the city center, To Je To is a youthful bar known for creative cocktails, craft beers, and a lively atmosphere, making it a favorite among both locals and tourists.

- Ghetto Club:

Situated in the heart of Split, Ghetto Club exudes an urban feel with DJ performances, live music, and theme parties, creating a dynamic and trendy nightlife destination.

- Vanilla Club:

As one of the premier nightclubs, Vanilla Club attracts a younger crowd with energetic EDM events, top DJs, and a stylish interior, making it a hotspot for nightlife enthusiasts.

- Tropic Club:

Beachside in Bacvice, Tropic Club offers a unique experience with vibrant parties, live music, and a mix of electronic and popular tunes, all set against the backdrop of the Adriatic Sea.

- Figa Food Bar:

Combining a trendy bar atmosphere with a focus on delicious food, Figa Food Bar is a popular spot for cocktails, craft beers, and a diverse menu of local and international dishes.

- Quasimodo Bar:

Nestled within Diocletian's Palace, Quasimodo Bar offers a historic setting with modern vibes. Enjoy cocktails with outdoor seating and views of the lively streets.

- Hemingway Bar:

Inspired by the famous writer, Hemingway Bar offers classic cocktails and a laid-back vintage ambiance—an ideal spot for a more sophisticated and relaxed evening.

- Toto's Burger Bar:

Known for delicious burgers, Toto's Burger Bar is also a trendy spot for craft beers and cocktails. It's a popular choice for those seeking a mix of great food and a vibrant atmosphere.

- Split Brewery:

Craft beer enthusiasts can explore locally brewed beers at Split Brewery, a cozy setting to sample different styles and socialize with locals.

These trendy bars and clubs contribute to Split's dynamic nightlife, offering a diverse range of experiences—from electronic music to live performances and craft cocktails. Explore the city's energetic evenings catered to various tastes and preferences.

Live music and performances

Discover the vibrant live music scene in Split with these popular venues offering diverse performances:

- Galerija Club:

Known for its diverse range of genres, including rock, pop, and electronic music, Galerija Club provides an intimate setting for live music, making it a favorite among locals and visitors.

- Jazzbina:

Located near Diocletian's Palace, Jazzbina is a cozy jazz club offering intimate live jazz performances—a perfect spot for those who appreciate the artistry of jazz music.

- Tropic Club:

In addition to its beach club ambiance, Tropic Club hosts live music, featuring bands and DJs across various genres. The beachside setting adds a unique touch to the live music experience.

- Vanilla Club:

While renowned for EDM events, Vanilla Club also hosts live music performances, creating an immersive experience with both local and international artists gracing the stage.

- Bacvice Beach Bars:

Several beach bars along Bacvice Beach present live music, ranging from acoustic sets to full bands, offering a relaxed atmosphere for enjoying performances, especially during the summer months.

- Central Cafe Bar:

Located in the city center, Central Caffe Bar frequently features live music, including acoustic performances and bands covering a variety of genres. The trendy atmosphere attracts both locals and tourists.

- Matejuska Harbor Bars:

Bars around Matejuska Harbor, near Diocletian's Palace, occasionally showcase live music performances, providing a charming waterfront setting for a delightful experience.

- O'Hara Music Club:

Situated near Split Riva, O'Hara Music Club is a dedicated live music venue hosting a range of performances, from rock and blues to alternative and indie music.

- Kocka:

Kocka, a unique cultural space in Split, hosts various events, including live music performances, art exhibitions, and theater productions—a dynamic venue embracing different forms of artistic expression.

- Vintage Industrial Bar:

Known for its alternative and rock club nights, Vintage Industrial Bar occasionally features live music events with performances by both local and international bands.

These venues contribute to the lively cultural scene in Split, offering music enthusiasts diverse settings, from beachfront bars to intimate jazz clubs and energetic nightclubs, to enjoy captivating live performances.

Chapter Six

Day Trips

Nearby Islands and Villages

Discover the enchanting destinations easily reachable from Split, serving as perfect starting points for exploration along the scenic Dalmatian coast:

- Brac Island:

A short ferry ride away, Brac beckons with its stunning beaches, including the famous Zlatni Rat. The town of Bol offers a picturesque harbor, historic sites, and vibrant nightlife.

- Hvar Island:

Accessible by ferry, Hvar, deemed one of the Adriatic's most beautiful islands, boasts a charming medieval town, vibrant nightlife, and the historic Hvar Fortress.

- Vis Island:

Known for its untouched beauty and secluded coves, Vis features charming streets and historical sites. Don't miss the Blue Cave in nearby Biševo, reachable by boat.

- Solta Island:

A peaceful retreat near Split, Solta offers picturesque villages like Stomorska and Maslinica, providing a serene escape and accessible by ferry.

- Trogir:

A UNESCO World Heritage site, Trogir is a historic town a short drive or boat ride away. Explore its medieval architecture, including the Cathedral of St. Lawrence and Kamerlengo Fortress.

- Kastela:

Nestled between Split and Trogir, the Kastela region boasts seven historic villages, each with its own charm, blending history, culture, and natural beauty.

- Primosten:

Located about 30 kilometers from Split, Primosten charms with narrow streets, medieval architecture, and a beautiful stone church. The town is renowned for its vineyards and the picturesque vineyard peninsula.

- Omis:

Surrounded by mountains and the Cetina River, Omis offers a mix of history and adventure. Explore the medieval fortress, take a boat tour on the Cetina River, or relax on sandy beaches.

- Brela:

Approximately 50 kilometers from Split, Brela allures with pristine beaches and crystal-clear waters, with Punta Rata beach standing out for its distinctive rock formations.

- Makarska:

Makarska, a vibrant town about 60 kilometers south of Split, boasts a lively promenade, beautiful beaches, and the impressive Biokovo Mountain as a backdrop. The Makarska Riviera offers various outdoor activities and picturesque villages.

These nearby islands and villages present a diverse array of experiences, from exploring historical sites to basking in the natural beauty of the Dalmatian coast. Whether your interests lean toward cultural exploration, beach relaxation, or outdoor adventures, the surroundings of Split offer a wealth of possibilities.

Excursions beyond Split

Embark on captivating excursions beyond Split, unveiling a realm of diverse experiences and attractions:

- Krka National Park:

An hour's drive unveils Krka National Park, renowned for its breathtaking waterfalls and lush landscapes. Hike scenic trails, swim beneath waterfalls, and revel in the park's rich flora and fauna.

- Plitvice Lakes National Park:

A 3-hour journey transports you to the UNESCO-listed Plitvice Lakes. Explore interconnected lakes, cascading waterfalls, and pristine forests via wooden boardwalks, immersing yourself in natural splendor.

- Sibenik:

Just an hour north, Sibenik beckons with medieval charm. Explore the UNESCO-listed Cathedral of St. James and wander the historic old town's narrow streets and stone houses.

- Dubrovnik:

Venture further (3.5 to 4 hours by car) to Dubrovnik, the "Pearl of the Adriatic." Walk the city walls, admire historic buildings, and absorb stunning views of the sea in this UNESCO World Heritage site.

- Trogir:

A short drive or boat trip brings you to Trogir, a UNESCO-listed gem with well-preserved medieval architecture. Roam narrow streets, visit the Cathedral of St. Lawrence, and gaze upon the Adriatic from Kamerlengo Fortress.

- Mostar (Bosnia and Herzegovina):

Explore the multicultural allure of Mostar, 2.5 to 3 hours away. Stari Most, the Old Bridge, and the historic old town showcase a rich tapestry of cultures and histories.

- Island Hopping:

Utilize Split as a gateway to Dalmatian coast islands like Hvar, Brac, Vis, Solta, and Korcula. Each island boasts distinct charm, beaches, and attractions.

- Cetina River Rafting:

Seek thrills with white-water rafting on the Cetina River, a 30-minute drive from Split. Navigate rapids, relish scenic vistas, and indulge in swimming and cliff jumping.

- Biokovo Mountain:

Drive or hike up Biokovo Mountain for panoramic views of the Adriatic coast. The Biokovo Nature Park harbors rare flora and fauna and stunning landscapes.

- Imotski:

Imotski, 1.5 to 2 hours away, captivates with its unique Blue and Red Lakes, karst formations displaying vibrant hues against the surrounding cliffs.

These excursions promise a medley of adventures, from natural wonders to cultural immersion and historical exploration. Whether your heart desires outdoor escapades, scenic panoramas, or cultural odysseys, the surrounding areas offer an array of delights for every taste.

Chapter Seven

Accommodation Guide

Hotels, Hostels, and Unique Stays

Split offers diverse accommodation options to cater to various preferences and budgets. Here are some noteworthy choices:

Hotels:

- Hotel Park Split:

Positioned near Bacvice Beach and the city center, Hotel Park Split provides luxurious accommodation with modern amenities. Enjoy elegant rooms, a rooftop terrace with a bar, and a spa for a lavish stay.

- Cornaro Hotel:

Situated in the heart of Split, the Cornaro Hotel blends contemporary design with historical elements. It features stylish rooms, a rooftop terrace boasting panoramic views, and a wellness center.

- Heritage Hotel Antique Split:

Nestled within Diocletian's Palace, this boutique hotel delivers a unique historical experience. Elegantly decorated rooms and the charming atmosphere of the Old Town create a distinctive stay.

- Radisson Blu Resort & Spa, Split:

A beachfront upscale resort offering spacious rooms, diverse dining options, a spa, and outdoor pools. It provides a luxurious retreat while maintaining proximity to the city center.

- Vestibul Palace:

Situated within Diocletian's Palace, Vestibul Palace is a boutique hotel blending modern and historical elements. Immerse yourself in the UNESCO-listed heritage while enjoying the courtyard.

Hostels:

- Hostel Split Backpackers:

Located in the city center, this social and lively hostel offers budget-friendly accommodation with dormitory-style rooms, catering to backpackers and those seeking a communal atmosphere.

- Design Hostel Goli & Bosi:

A stylish hostel near the ferry terminal, Goli & Bosi provides modern design, comfortable dorms, and private rooms. Its vibrant common areas contribute to a friendly atmosphere.

- Tchaikovsky Hostel Split:

Set in a historic building in the Old Town, Tchaikovsky Hostel offers a mix of dormitory and private rooms. With a communal kitchen and lounge, it provides a cozy atmosphere.

- Split Guesthouse & Hostel:

This budget-friendly hostel in the city center offers simple and clean accommodations, making it an excellent choice for travelers seeking a convenient base to explore Split.

Unique Stays:

- Diocletian Wine House:

A unique experience offering stylish apartments within Diocletian's Palace. Enjoy modern amenities while being immersed in the historical ambiance.

- Sleep Split:

Boutique-style apartments in various city center locations, Sleep Split offers contemporary design and a personalized stay for a comfortable experience.

- Boban Luxury Suites:

Located near Bacvice Beach, Boban Luxury Suites provides elegant suites with a touch of luxury. It offers a peaceful retreat close to both the beach and the city center.

- Villa Marjela:

A charming villa in a quiet neighborhood, Villa Marjela offers cozy rooms, a garden, and a terrace for a relaxed residential experience.

Whether opting for the luxury of a hotel, the sociability of a hostel, or the charm of a unique stay, Split caters to diverse preferences and travel styles.

Budget-Friendly Options

For budget-conscious travelers, Split offers a variety of affordable accommodation options, ranging from budget hotels to hostels and guesthouses. Here are some budget-friendly choices:

Budget Hotels:

- Hotel Jadran:

Conveniently located near the city center and Bacvice Beach, Hotel Jadran provides simple and affordable rooms. It serves as a practical base for exploring Split's attractions without straining your budget.

- Hotel Dalmina:

Situated slightly outside the city center, Hotel Dalmina offers comfortable and reasonably priced rooms. The hotel provides free parking and easy access to public transportation, making it a practical choice for budget travelers.

- Hotel Consul:

Nestled in a residential area, Hotel Consul is a budget-friendly option with basic yet clean and comfortable rooms. It caters to those seeking affordable accommodation with straightforward access to the city center.

Hostels and guesthouses:

- Hostel Emanuel:

Centrally located, Hostel Emanuel provides budget-friendly dormitory-style rooms with shared facilities. It offers a simple and social environment, making it suitable for backpackers and budget-conscious travelers.

- Adriatic Hostel:

Positioned near the ferry terminal and the city center, Adriatic Hostel offers budget-friendly dormitories and private rooms. It's an ideal choice for those on a tight budget who still want a convenient location.

- Design Hostel 101 Dalmatinac:

Situated close to the beach, this stylish hostel offers affordable dormitory accommodations with a modern design. It provides a lively atmosphere and is within walking distance of popular attractions.

Guesthouses and Apartments:

- Apartment Mira:

Found in a residential area, Apartment Mira offers self-catering accommodation at affordable rates. It's a good option for budget travelers seeking more privacy and flexibility.

- Guesthouse Vrlic:

Located near the city center, Guesthouse Vrlic provides budget-friendly rooms with simple furnishings. It offers a convenient and affordable stay for travelers exploring Split on a budget.

- Apartments Gajeta:

Apartments Gajeta offers budget-friendly apartment accommodation in the heart of Split. It's a suitable choice for those who prefer self-catering and want to save on dining expenses.

These budget-friendly options provide affordable and comfortable stays, allowing travelers to maximize their visit to Split without exceeding their budget. Whether opting for a budget hotel, hostel, or guesthouse,

Split offers various choices to suit different preferences and travel styles.

Chapter Eight

Practical Information

Currency and Banking

Discovering the financial landscape of Split, Croatia, is a key aspect of planning your journey.

Here's what you need to know:

- Currency:

Croatian Kuna (HRK) is the official currency, denoted by "kn" or "HRK." Banknotes and coins come in various denominations.

- Banking Hours:

Banks operate Monday through Friday; some are open Saturdays. Hours vary, but usually start in the morning and end early in the afternoon. ATMs offer cash access outside of these hours.

- ATMs:

Conveniently located throughout Split, especially in central areas and near attractions.

Accept major international cards for Kuna withdrawals.

- Credit Cards:

Visa and MasterCard are widely accepted in hotels, restaurants, and shops. Carry cash for smaller purchases or places without card facilities.

- Currency Exchange:

Available at banks, exchange offices, and some hotels. Stick to official offices for fair rates; avoid street exchanges.

- Tipping:

Customary in restaurants and for services; 10-15% tip common. Some places include a service charge; check your bill.

- Currency Restrictions:

There are no specific limits for travelers. Stay informed about regulations from local authorities or your bank.

- Banking Services:

Banks offer international transfers and currency assistance in addition to exchange and ATM services.

- Traveler's Cheques:

Less common, but some banks may accept them. We recommend relying on cash and cards for ease.

- Language:

English is widely spoken, simplifying communication at banks and tourist spots.

Inform your bank of your travel plans beforehand to avoid transaction issues. Check current exchange rates and fees for informed financial decisions during your stay.

Safety Tips

Ensuring a safe and enjoyable visit to Split involves staying informed and following basic safety guidelines.

Here are some essential safety tips:

- General Safety:

Split is generally safe, but remain vigilant in crowded areas. Watch your belongings and be cautious of pickpockets.

- Emergency Numbers:

Know the emergency number: 112. Dial for police, medical aid, or firefighting services. Familiarize yourself with local emergency contacts.

- Public Transportation:

Opt for licensed taxis or ride-sharing. Beware of unofficial taxis and keep an eye on belongings when using buses.

- Currency and Values:

Use secure pouches for documents and valuables. Avoid displaying large sums of cash in public.

- Beach Safety:

Watch your belongings at the beach. Be cautious of currents and follow lifeguard guidelines.

- Health Precautions:

Have travel insurance that covers medical expenses. Carry medications and know the nearest medical facilities. Stay hydrated, especially in the summer.

- Local laws and customs:

Know and respect local laws. Croatia has strict drug laws. Respect customs and cultural sensitivities.

- Weather Awareness:

Stay hydrated in hot summers. Follow local advisories during extreme weather.

- Use reputable services:

Choose licensed providers for activities. Check reviews and seek recommendations.

- Travel Insurance:

Consider comprehensive travel insurance for medical emergencies and trip cancellations.

- Cultural Sensitivity:

Dress modestly at religious sites. Be aware of local traditions and etiquette.

- COVID-19 Precautions:

Stay informed about travel advisories and health guidelines. Follow local regulations and practice good hygiene.

With awareness, respect, and basic precautions, your visit to Split can be both secure and enjoyable. Trust your instincts and seek local assistance if needed.

Chapter Nine

Local Insights

Interviews with locals

Exploring Split through local interviews offers a unique lens into the city's culture. Consider these questions to delve into the community's insights:

- Introduction:

Can you introduce yourself? What's your name, and how long have you called Split home?

- Local Life:

What aspects of Split Life do you cherish the most? Are there unique local elements that you find particularly enjoyable?

- Favorite Spots:

Share your go-to places or activities in Split. Any hidden gems or local spots you'd recommend to visitors?

- Cultural Traditions:

Highlight significant cultural traditions or festivals in Split. How do locals partake in and celebrate these events?

- Cuisine and Dining:

What local dishes or specialties should visitors try in Split? Any favorite eateries or markets you'd suggest?

- Community Bond:

Describe the sense of community in Split. Are there events that bring people together?

- Changes Over Time:

Have you witnessed notable changes in Split? How has the city evolved, and what's the impact on the community?

- Tourism Impact:

Considering tourism's role in Split's economy, how do you view its impact on the local community? Any positives or negatives?

- Outdoor Activities:

With Split's reputation for outdoor pursuits, what activities or sports do you enjoy in and around the city?

- Local Challenges:

Every community faces challenges. In your view, what challenges does Split currently face, and what solutions do you propose?

- Pride in Heritage:

Do you feel a strong tie to Split's historical and cultural heritage? How does it shape the community's identity?

- Advice for Visitors:

If you could guide visitors to Split, what advice would you offer? Any insider tips or recommendations?

- Future Hopes:

What are your aspirations for Split's future? Are there any specific changes or developments you'd like to see?

- Local Art and Culture:

Describe Split's local art and cultural scene. Any standout artists, musicians, or cultural events that capture your attention?

- Sense of Belonging:

What does "home" signify to you in Split? How would you describe the sense of belonging within this community?

Approach locals with genuine interest and respect, adapting questions based on context. Embrace the diverse stories and perspectives each person brings, fostering a deeper appreciation for Split's rich cultural tapestry.

Hidden gems and insiders

Unveiling hidden gems and local tips can elevate your Split experience. Consider these lesser-known spots and insider recommendations from the locals:

- Varos District:

Wander through Varos, a charming district with narrow streets and historic houses. a tranquil getaway from the busy metropolitan core.

- Sustipan Park:

Enjoy breathtaking sea views at Sustipan Park. A tranquil haven on the peninsula's southwestern tip, perfect for picnics and relaxation.

- Fruit's Square (Vocni Trg.):

Immerse yourself in the local atmosphere at Fruit's Square. A vibrant, small square surrounded by cafes is ideal for people-watching and sipping coffee.

- Caffe Bar Vidilica:

Head to Caffe Bar Vidilica on Marjan Hill for panoramic views. A hidden gem provides the perfect setting for a sunset drink.

- Museum of Senses:

Experience the interactive Museum of Senses near Diocletian's Palace. A playful exploration of sensory perception.

- Pazar Market:

Dive into local culture at Pazar Market, near Diocletian's Palace. Sample fresh produce and homemade goods in this lively market.

- Marmont Street:

Explore Marmont Street, a bustling pedestrian area with shops and cafes. A vibrant place to stroll and soak up the lively atmosphere.

- Kresimirova Street Art Alley:

Discover the artistic side of Split at Kresimirova Street Art Alley. Colorful street art adorns this hidden gem.

- Jupiter's Temple Crypt:

Uncover the Crypt of Jupiter's Temple beneath Diocletian's Palace. A lesser-known historical site with well-preserved columns.

- Fish Market (Riba Market):

Indulge in local seafood at the fish market near the green market. Take in the maritime culture of the city.

- Obojena Svjetlost Bookstore:

Book lovers can escape to Obojena Svjetlost, a cozy bookstore with a diverse collection. a peaceful haven away from the bustle of the city.

- Kasjuni Beach:

Opt for the quieter Kasjuni Beach, which is surrounded by pine trees. A secluded and peaceful alternative to the popular Bacvice Beach.

- Kastelet Beach and Church:

Enjoy serenity at Kastelet Beach on Marjan Hill, accompanied by a picturesque church. A calm area away from the crowd.

- Marjan Staircase:

Exercise with a view; climb the Marjan Staircase for panoramic vistas of Split and nearby islands.

- Art Bottega Studio:

Art enthusiasts can explore Art Bottega Studio, a hidden art haven near Diocletian's Palace, showcasing unique pieces by local artists.

These hidden gems promise a more authentic exploration of Split, allowing you to uncover the city's lesser-known treasures.

Recommendations

- Explore Diocletian's Palace:

Immerse yourself in the heart of Split's history by wandering through the ancient streets of Diocletian's Palace. Don't miss the central square, Peristyle.

- Take a Stroll Along the Riva Promenade:

Experience the vibrant atmosphere of Split's waterfront at the Riva Promenade. Enjoy a leisurely walk, grab a coffee, and soak in the lively surroundings.

- Climb Marjan Hill:

Hike or walk to the top of Marjan Hill for breathtaking views of Split, the Adriatic Sea, and the neighboring islands. This verdant park provides a calm haven.

- Visit Bacvice Beach:

Relax at Bacvice Beach, known for its sandy shores and clear waters. This is a well-liked location for swimming, tanning, and relaxing at coastal cafes.

- Try local cuisine:

Delight your taste buds with Dalmatian cuisine at traditional Konoba restaurants. Savor dishes like pasticada, peka, and fresh seafood. Explore local markets for regional produce.

- Day Trip to the Islands:

Embark on a ferry or boat tour to nearby islands such as Hvar, Brac, or Vis. Each island boasts a unique charm, beautiful beaches, and historical sites.

- See a play at the National Theatre of Croatia:

Immerse yourself in arts and culture by checking the schedule for performances at the Croatian National Theatre. Enjoy a play, opera, or ballet in a historic setting.

- Experience Split's Nightlife:

Dive into the city's vibrant nightlife scene by exploring trendy bars, clubs, and cafes. Many establishments line the city center and waterfront.

- Take a Walking Tour:

Enrich your understanding of the city with a guided walking tour. Learn about Split's history, architecture, and local anecdotes, covering landmarks like Diocletian's Palace and the Cathedral of St. Domnius.

- Visit the Mestrovic Gallery:

Explore the works of sculptor Ivan Mestrovic at the Mestrovic Gallery. Housed in a villa with a sculpture garden, the gallery provides a captivating artistic experience.

- Relax at Bene Beach:

Discover the tranquility of Bene Beach, nestled on the northern side of Marjan Hill. This secluded spot, surrounded by pine trees, offers a peaceful retreat.

- Attend a local festival or event:

Check the events calendar for festivals and events during your visit. Split hosts various cultural, music, and food festivals throughout the year.

- Discover the Underground Cellars:

Take a tour of Diocletian's Palace underground cellars, showcasing the architectural brilliance of the palace.

- Explore Trogir:

Enjoy a day trip to the UNESCO-listed town of Trogir. Wander through medieval streets, visit historical sites, and soak in the charming atmosphere.

- Engage with locals:

Connect with locals at cafes, markets, or parks. Their insights often lead to hidden gems and unique experiences.

These recommendations offer a blend of cultural, historical, culinary, and leisurely experiences in Split. Enjoy your visit to this vibrant and historically rich city!

Chapter Ten

Split for Every Season

The Best Times to Visit

Determining the best time to visit Split, Croatia, depends on your preferences for weather, crowd levels, and activities. Here's a breakdown for different seasons:

- Spring (April to June):

Ideal for mild weather and blooming nature.

Less crowded for exploring historical sites and outdoor activities.

- Summer (July to August):

High tourist season with hot and dry weather.

Lively atmosphere with events, festivals, and outdoor concerts.

Crowded, especially at popular attractions.

- Fall (September to October):

Pleasant weather with warm temperatures lingering into September.

Good for beach activities with warmer sea temperatures.

Less crowded, offering a relaxed atmosphere.

- Winter (November to March):

Off-peak season with cool and rainy weather.

Suitable for exploring cultural attractions and local life.

There are fewer crowds compared to other seasons.

- Shoulder Seasons (April, May, September, and October):

Considered optimal for a balanced experience.

Pleasant weather with fewer tourists.

Suitable for outdoor activities and city exploration.

- Special Events:

Summer festivals like the Split Summer Festival in July and August offer cultural performances.

Local celebrations and festivals occur throughout the year, providing unique experiences.

- Outdoor Activities:

Spring and fall are ideal for outdoor activities like hiking, cycling, and island exploration.

Comfortable weather and picturesque landscapes during these seasons.

- Sea Temperature:

It is warmest in the summer for swimming and water activities.

Still enjoyable in shoulder seasons.

- Avoiding Crowds:

Shoulder seasons are optimal for exploring attractions without large crowds.

- Local Cuisine:

Local cuisine is available year-round, with diverse offerings and availability in the shoulder seasons.

Ultimately, your choice depends on personal preferences. Whether you seek the energy of summer or the tranquility of shoulder seasons, Split has something to offer at different times of the year.

Seasonal Activities

Seasonal activities in Split offer diverse experiences throughout the year. Here are suggestions for activities based on each season:

Spring (April to June):

- Explore Diocletian's Palace: Enjoy the historic streets of Diocletian's Palace in mild spring weather with fewer crowds.

- Marjan Hill Hiking: Take a hike up Marjan Hill to witness blooming nature and panoramic views of Split and the Adriatic Sea.

- Attend Cultural Events: Embrace the season's cultural events, including local performances, art exhibitions, and music festivals.

Summer (July to August):

- Relax on Bacvice Beach: Bask in the sun and swim at Bacvice Beach, the favored city beach during the warm summer months.

- Island Hopping: Explore nearby islands like Hvar, Brac, and Vis with frequent boat services in the summer.
- Attend Open-Air Concerts: Enjoy open-air concerts and events on the Riva Promenade or within Diocletian's Palace in the warm summer evenings.

Fall (September to October):

- Wine Tasting in the Dalmatian Hinterland: Experience the grape harvest season with wine tasting in the Dalmatian Hinterland.
- Olive Harvest Experience: Participate in olive harvesting activities for a unique insight into local agricultural practices.
- Cultural Tours: Visit historical sites and museums in pleasant fall weather with fewer crowds.

Winter (November to March):

- Explore Indoor Attractions: Visit museums, galleries, and historical sites such as the Mestrovic Gallery and Split City Museum during the cooler months.

- Experience Local Cuisine: Savor hearty local dishes, including pasticada, and other comfort foods in cozy restaurants.
- Attend Winter Festivals: Immerse yourself in the festive atmosphere during winter festivals and Christmas markets in the city center.

Throughout the year:
- Walking Tours: Explore the city on foot with guided walking tours, discovering historical landmarks and hidden gems.
- Water Activities: Enjoy kayaking or paddleboarding, ideal for various seasons, especially during mild weather.
- Culinary Experiences: Taste local specialties, join cooking classes, or embark on food tours to experience Dalmatian cuisine.
- Cycling: Rent a bike to explore scenic surroundings, including Marjan Hill and nearby coastal areas.

- Photography Tours: Capture the beauty of Split with photography tours, showcasing the best spots and angles.

Split provides a diverse range of activities, allowing visitors to tailor their experiences based on seasonal preferences. Whether you are interested in cultural events, outdoor adventures, or culinary delights, each season offers unique opportunities in this dynamic city.

Conclusion

Closing the pages of the "Split Travel Guide 2024," I felt immense satisfaction after exploring one of Croatia's captivating cities. Split, a city woven with rich history, vibrant culture, and stunning landscapes, has been an enchanting canvas for the travel experiences we've vividly depicted.

Throughout this guide, I navigated the ancient streets of Diocletian's Palace, uncovering the stories embedded in its UNESCO World Heritage Site stones. From lively markets to the warmth of Adriatic beaches, every corner revealed a layer of Split's fascinating past.

The Riva Promenade, pulsating at the heart of the city, became a hub of activity where locals and visitors converged, sharing in the joy of life. I delved into dynamic nightlife, exploring bars, clubs, and cultural events that animate the city after sundown. The guide steered us through the intricate labyrinth of streets, leading to hidden gems, local hangouts, and panoramic viewpoints that revealed the city's true essence.

My journey extended to neighboring islands, each offering a unique charm. From the serene beauty of Hvar to the rugged landscapes of Brac, the nearby islands complemented the allure of Split.

Throughout the seasons, from spring's vitality to winter celebrations, I discovered that Split is a city that embraces visitors year-round. Insights into the best times to visit ensured every traveler found their preferred atmosphere.

Practical advice, from budget-friendly accommodations to safety tips and cultural etiquette, equipped readers. I explored the culinary scene, guiding readers to savor authentic Dalmatian tastes. Travelers were encouraged to engage with locals, attend festivals, and immerse themselves in the community.

If I conclude this guide, I hope readers feel empowered and inspired to explore Split's soul.

Not just a destination, Split offers an immersive experience that leaves an indelible mark on hearts.

May this guide be a companion to the curious traveler, offering insights, recommendations, and anticipation for the wonders in Split. As the sun sets over the Adriatic, may every reader carry echoes of Split's stories, the taste of its cuisine, and the warmth of its hospitality.

In the spirit of exploration and discovery, I bid you farewell, dear reader, with the hope that your journey through Split is as enriching and unforgettable as the words within these pages. Until we meet again under the Dalmatian sun, happy travels, and may your adventures be filled with the magic that is Split.

Useful Maps

When navigating Split, having the right maps can greatly enhance your visit. Here are essential maps to make your exploration seamless:

- Split City Map:

Navigate streets, alleys, and landmarks with this detailed map featuring key points of interest and public transportation routes.

- Diocletian's Palace Map:

Explore Diocletian's Palace with ease using this dedicated map, which guides you through the Peristyle, basements, and historical sites.

- Marjan Hill Map:

For hikers, a map of Marjan Hill's trails, viewpoints, and attractions is essential.

- Public Transportation Map:

Efficiently move around Split with a map showcasing bus routes and schedules.

- Ferry Route Map:

Plan island-hopping adventures with a map outlining ferry routes and timetables.

- Beach Map:

Find your perfect beach spot using a map highlighting various beaches in and around Split.

- Cycling Route Map:

Cyclists can enjoy mapped routes around Split, covering Marjan Hill and coastal areas.

- Restaurant and Cafe Guide:

Discover culinary gems with a map indicating recommended eateries.

- Shopping District Map:

Shop wisely by exploring the main districts and popular stores on this map.

- Museum and Gallery Map:

Immerse yourself in Split's culture with a map detailing museum and gallery locations.

- Parking Map:

Driving? Use this map to find parking areas and facilities.

- WiFi Hotspot Map:

Stay connected on the go with a map of WiFi hotspots in public areas and cafes.

- Emergency Services Map:

Stay safe with a map showing hospitals, pharmacies, and police stations.

- Tourist Information Center Map:

Get guidance at your fingertips with a map of tourist information center locations.

- City Event Calendar:

Plan around special occasions with a calendar of city events and festivals.

Obtain these maps from tourist centers, hotels, or official city websites to maximize your time in Split. Bursting with information, they ensure a perplexity-free exploration of the city.

Map of Split

Language Basics

For a smoother experience in Split, Croatia, familiarize yourself with these handy Croatian phrases:

Hello:

- Croatian: Bok (pronounced "bohk").

Good morning:

- Croatian: Dobro jutro (pronounced "doh-broh YOO-troh").

Good afternoon or good day:

- Croatian: Dobar dan (pronounced "DOH-bahr dahn").

Good evening:

- Croatian: Dobra večer (pronounced "DOH-brah VEH-chehr").

Good night:

- Croatian: Laku noć (pronounced "LAH-koo notch").

Yes:

- Croatian: Da (pronounced "dah").

No:

- Croatian: Ne (pronounced "neh")

Thank you:

- Croatian: Hvala (pronounced "WAH-lah")

You're welcome:

- Croatian: Nema na čemu (pronounced "NEH-mah nah CHEH-moo").

Excuse me, I'm sorry:

- Croatian: Oprosti (pronounced "OH-pros-tee"), informal
- Croatian: Oprostite (pronounced "OH-pros-tee-te"). formal or addressing multiple people

Please:

- Croatian: Molim (pronounced "MOH-leem").

Do you speak English?

- Croatian: Govorite li engleski? (pronounced "GOH-voh-ree-teh lee ENG-les-kee")

I don't understand:

- Croatian: Ne razumijem (pronounced "neh rah-ZOO-mee-yem").

How much is this?

- Croatian: Koliko ovo košta? (pronounced "KOH-lee-koh OH-vo KOH-stah?")

Where is...?:

- Croatian: Gdje je...? (pronounced "gd yeh yeh...?")

Bathroom/Toilet:

- Croatian: WC (pronounced "vay-say")

I need help.

- Croatian: Trebam pomoć (pronounced "TREH-bahm POH-mohtsch")

I'm lost:

- Croatian: Izgubio/izgubila sam se (male/female) (pronounced "EEZ-goo-bio/EEZ-goo-bee-lah sahm seh")

Cheers!:

- Croatian: Živjeli (pronounced "ZHEE-vee-lee").

Goodbye:

- Croatian: Doviđenja (pronounced "doh-VEE-jeh-nyah").

Utilize these phrases to connect with locals and enhance your experience in Split. While English is widely spoken, making an effort in Croatian can add a burst of authenticity to your interactions.

Printed in Great Britain
by Amazon